MEA
Michigan Education Association

MW00745155

800-292-1934

August 1, 2017

Welcome to MEA's 2017 Summer Leadership Conference. To help you be a leader in these challenging and changing times, we are pleased to provide you with this book by Randy Fox.

We know it will help you to Excite, Engage and Empower yourself as a leader as well as your members.

Enjoy the conference!

Sincerely,

Gretchen Dziadosz
Executive Director

Affiliated with the National Education Association

A Leader Worth Following

Become a leader of quality, character & integrity

Randy Fox

TABLE OF CONTENTS

DEDICATION

To my grandfather,
Fred Aellig (Poor Fred)
who taught me the importance of being
a man who works hard, is honest,
wise, kind, trustworthy, humble
and someone worthy of following.

I miss you, and will always strive
to reflect your wisdom
and love to the world.

A Leader Worth Following

PROLOGUE

The Lion has long been recognized as the King of the Jungle. No other animal deserves that honor. The Lion is the strength and stability of the Animal Kingdom. His long, golden mane, his exquisite bearing and his indomitable presence wherever he goes is legendary.

No other animal can match his grace and power.

The elephant is larger but lacks the leadership image. The hippo is the most dangerous to man but again is woefully short on elegance. The hyena is a scavenger and not worthy of a reputable following.

The monkey is a clown, the tiger is too menacing, the cheetah is one-dimensional, the gazelle is too afraid, the wildebeest is too ugly, the crocodile is water-limited and the chameleon is too compromising.

No, it is the Lion.

Stately, majestic, revered and protective, no other animal can match his grace, beauty and reputation and no other animal dares to challenge him.

The Lion is the Leader Worth Following.

If business were run with Lions at the helm they would be profitable in every way both in the bottom line of excellence and the foundational value of ethics.

A leader worth following must have the moral basics, the believability in image and reputation, and the bearing of a champion.

A leader must be a Lion.

The Lion is the leader worth following.

CHAPTER ONE

The Motivator *is* the Message

**"If you don't believe the messenger,
you won't believe the message."** Barry Posner

People don't follow a cause, a company or a goal... *they follow you.*

A great example comes from the spiritual realm.

The Bible is a book about characters *of character.* No one had more integrity than Jesus, and his devotion to moral excellence was the foundation for the allegiance of his closest followers, the disciples.

Except for Judas, of course.

He was so blinded by greed that he couldn't see beyond it. As a result, he was one of the few people in the company of Jesus who failed to be dramatically influenced for the better.

But, the rest of the apostles became a Who's Who of religious renown. To this day, Peter is the foundation of the church.

John, who penned one of the four Gospels and two Epistles was also acclaimed for writing the Book of Revelation. The list of leaders from those early days is like a biblical All-Star team...James, Matthew, Nathaniel, Andrew, Philip and of course, Thomas.

Remarkably ten out of the twelve disciples died a martyr's death.

The question looms large...why?

Because they passionately believed in the message of their leader. That begs a second question: Why did they believe so strongly, even to the point of death, in his mission on earth?

The answer is stunningly clear. Because they believed in *Him*.

They believed in Jesus with all their heart, with all their soul and with all their mind.

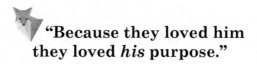 **"Because they loved him they loved *his* purpose."**

That is *a leader worth following*. It was true 2,000 years ago and it is still true today.

In our modern era, nothing has changed. The same principles still apply today. A reason organizations falter is because there is a lack of core respect and admiration for many of the executives involved in leadership.

During many of the infamous corporate scandals, such as Enron, Tyco, AIG, or Lehman Brothers, it was sad to see the CEO's and their Vice-Presidents being led away in handcuffs.

Watching these men with their grim faces and bowed heads being put into police cars was disheartening to me. All these companies had high hopes, with employees and shareholders excited about both the purposes of their work and potential benefits from their hard work.

But, it all came down to this: A lack of character at the core of leaders *not* worth following.

Simple as that.

"Nearly all men can stand adversity, but if you want to test a man's character, give him power."
Abraham Lincoln

So, let's lay some groundwork here. What are the top <u>five</u> assets of *a leader worth following*?

It's a *subjective* question but I think we can agree on a few of them here. Let's give it a shot.

1. They always do the right thing

A leader worth following does not look at what is best for him or her, they look at what is *ethical* in every situation. It's getting rarer and rarer to find individuals and companies that value doing the right thing over financial profit, but, when you find a leader who is passionate about that premise, they are the one who is worth following.

2. They care for people

Putting others first is a remarkable quality that defines a great leader. When you find one that believes in that concept you know they will always look out for *your* best interests as their employee, client or partner.

3. They are fair and just

Many times in the course of the year a situation will rise up and challenge the point of justice in a tough time. A leader who knows how to mete out the foundational fairness with wisdom is your kind of leader.

4. They are honest

Honesty is not only the best policy it is the only attribute that will bring integrity to every working situation. *A leader worth following* is totally and completely trustworthy, always. They speak the truth, live the truth and inspire it!

5. They are passionate about taking personal responsibility

Workplaces are saturated with, *"The Blame Game."* Everyone wants to point the finger at someone else when something goes wrong. But, a great leader always looks at his or her role in any mistake and admits their part in it. Mentors who do that will always earn the respect and trust of others. In short, they possess uncommon humility.

"One of the truest tests of integrity is its blunt refusal to be compromised." Chinua Achebe

Enter a high school volleyball player named Emmee Ashby. She and her team were engaged in a close game with another school and a hard hit ball from her opponents came flying over the net and landed out of bounds.

The referee ruled the point to Emmee's team, giving them a 23-22 lead late in the crucial contest.

However.

Emmee went to the referee and admitted that the ball had grazed her on its way out of bounds, something the rules man had failed to see. He reversed his decision and the score now favored the other team, 23-22.

Was this an act of integrity on the young girl's part or was it a foolish choice that put her and her team in jeopardy of losing the game?

Her coach commended her for the integrity she displayed. I praise her, too. She knew the right thing to do and she did it.

Emmee was not just a leader on her team she was *a leader worth following.*

The question screams at us: **"Why would integrity and character be a preferred method of foundational leadership over the financial bottom line where company and individual profits are king?"**

The answer is found in the hearts of men and women everywhere.

In a nationwide survey of long-term marriages that survived divorce, we find the truth. When asked the most important ingredient for marital stability the answer was more than a little surprising...

The ability to communicate effectively?

Although important, that was not the #1 answer.

Understanding each other?

Nope.

Sexual attraction?

Wrong again.

Give up?

Here it is, and to be honest, it even surprised me...

The secret behind successful marriages was the ability to make each other feel *safe.*

As long as that was ongoing the union not only survived, it flourished.

That's why adultery is so devastating. It undercuts the trust needed to protect the romantic heart and shatters the fragile foundation of two people who are vulnerable after giving their hand to each other at the altar.

The ability to feel **safe.** Never underestimate it in your business, organization or personal leadership, either. The world is extremely competitive, with everyone trying to get an edge over the next guy. When an environment like that exists, then the basic building blocks of decency such as honesty, personal responsibility, humility, integrity and unselfishness are replaced with egoism, narcissism, pride, greed and cheating.

Enron and AIG didn't collapse because they operated too fairly. They fell apart because too many of their leaders substituted things that should have been decent, just, and laden with character, with materialism and profits at all costs.

Character makes people and companies feel *safe*. When you are doing the right thing there is an inner corporate and personal peace that accompanies it.

"The reconnection of society, economy and ethics is a project we cannot postpone." Michael D. Higgins

The safety of society, business, corporate leadership and the employees who work for them depends on it.

This is why integrity and character are stronger motivations than greed and financial profitability in business. This is what leaders need to do to give people inspiration and hope.

A great example from a personal story:

Nearly 20 years ago I worked at a printing company as the Customer Service Manager. My leader was the President of the company, and a successful businessman. His name is Steve McGrath.

He came to work each day with a passion to do great work, with a smile on his face, and a true desire to please our customers. He was strategic, creative, intelligent and decisive. Everything you would want from a leader.

That just begins to describe Steve. The best part of Steve was his care for people, his character, and his unwavering foundational ethics. He was honest. People trusted him.

I was a young, aspiring leader, in my mid twenties at the time. He became an instant mentor for me.

Steve would walk the entire facility every day, smile, shake hands and call every employee by name.

He didn't just offer them employment, he offered them himself.

He cared for them. He also cared for our customers.

If a client wasn't satisfied, in any way, Steve would call them, or more often than not, he would go visit them in person. He would give them the entire project at no charge if that is what it took to regain their loyalty.

He honored his word, even if it cost thousands of dollars in the process. And sometimes it did.

What did I do?

The same thing the other 100 plus employees did.

We followed.

In just two fast years we grew our sales and profits by over 100%.

Why did we achieve 100% growth?

You may think it was because we raised prices.

Nope.

Or maybe the obvious answer is because we cut costs.

Not one lay off. We actually hired people.

It was because Steve, and all of us, put people first. *He* was our motivator.

The message was to serve with integrity.

And that is what we did.

I still keep in touch with Steve. He is the same man of integrity today. Caring. Trustworthy. Compassionate.

He was a key mentor in shaping the type of leader I have become. I am forever grateful for who he is and his role in helping me be who I am.

"If you have integrity, nothing else matters.
If you don't have integrity, nothing else matters."
Alan K. Simpson

This is *why* we need leaders worth following.

Are you that leader?

CHAPTER TWO

The Visionary Leader

People follow leaders because leaders *lead*. There is somewhere worthy to go. Visionary leaders are strategic, optimistic, decisive and courageous.

Most people are too consumed with their past to see the potential of their future. Most of our past is for a brief learning period, not an ignition key to our potential.

In fact, the best way to have a successful future is to *erase* our past.

This is standard operating procedure for the visionary leader.

"The visionary starts with a clean sheet of paper, and re-imagines the world." Malcolm Gladwell

A status quo guy loves details on a white board and stays put. A visionary's dream is to erase the board and create from there. Our history has been full of these remarkable men and women.

The Wright Brothers owned a bicycle shop and envisioned one with wings. Hence, the airplane was born.

Henry Ford imagined a vehicle with wheels instead of an animal with hooves. Edison and Tesla said, "Let there be light," and it happened.

In 1959, the Green Bay Packers were the worst team in pro football. They hired a man from Brooklyn who had never coached at the pro or college level. His name was Vince Lombardi.

He took out his eraser and started from scratch in rebuilding his hapless team. From his bench he made Bart Starr his quarterback and he moved Paul Hornung to running back alongside Jimmy Taylor.

Lombardi cut several players from the losing roster and made some trades and in one year he took a team that had been 1-11 in 1958 to a winning record. The following year he took them to the NFL Championship game where they were edged out by the Philadelphia Eagles, 17-13.

He promised his players, "We will never lose a championship game again."

They never did.

Over the next seven years, this visionary leader won five NFL Championships and two Super Bowls. He sent twelve of his players to the Hall of Fame, was inducted there himself, and the coveted Super Bowl award bears his name, "The Vince Lombardi Trophy."

One man. One visionary. One white board with a clean slate.

**"Have a vision.
It is the ability to see the invisible.
If you can see the invisible,
you can achieve the impossible."** Shiv Khera

When a young senator from Massachusetts announced his intention to run for the President of the United States in January, 1960, not many people gave him a chance.

He was too young, a Roman Catholic, virtually unknown outside his home state with an undistinguished record in the Senate. He also had a thick New England dialect with a staccato delivery never heard before from the campaign platform.

He was also running against an incumbent Vice-President who served his Republican leader, Dwight D. Eisenhower, admirably for eight years. He faced a potent slate of Democratic opponents including Adlai Stevenson, Lyndon Johnson, Hubert Humphrey and Stuart Symington.

The young senator had little chance to win, or so it seemed to the status quo people who evaluated his campaign.

But, he and his team of visionary leaders, all young men who were new to national politics had a blank white board to work with here. They started from scratch and designed a Presidential campaign unlike any other in the history of politics.

The crafters of this revolutionary plan were Lawrence O'Brien, Kenneth O'Donnell, Theodore Sorenson, Pierre Salinger and Robert F. Kennedy.

The young senator, of course, was John Fitzgerald Kennedy.

On November 8, 1960, against all odds, he was elected the 35th President of the United States.

No way.

Never say those two words to a visionary leader.

John Kennedy had the "eyes" to see the invisible and was able to achieve the impossible.

What are the main characteristics of a successful visionary in any field?

When it comes to lists, I prefer groups of five:

1. The "box"

Most people work and live within the "box," the normal lifestyle and beliefs of societal norms. Some people venture outside the box and take a risk now and then. A visionary asks the stunning question, "What box?"

People that work with a blank slate also work with an invisible box. They don't concern themselves with boundaries or limitations. Therefore, they are free to ideate and operate with no-holds barred.

2. A singular critic

The Visionary marches to his or her own drummer. They pound away until their beat arrives at their dream and becomes a reality. They don't worry or fret about the doubts and scoffing of others. They are a singular critic made up of themselves.

They say *who*, they say *why*, they say *where* and they say *when* until the _how_ becomes a _what_.

Abraham Lincoln, like all of us, had many critics. Here are his words regarding their opinions:

**"If I were to try to read, much less answer,
all the attacks made on me,
this shop might as well be closed for any other
business. I do the very best I know how -
the very best I can; and I mean to
keep doing so until the end."** Abraham Lincoln

3. The "eyes" have it

A Visionary sees things most people don't see. Remember the dramatic scene in the movie, "Bugsy" when Warren Beatty's character, Ben Siegel was standing out in the desert and imagined Las Vegas?

Great visual of what happens when a Visionary sees the dream for the first time. Most people would have used their eyes and seen a desert. Siegel used his and saw a whole new world. If he were still alive and visited Las Vegas today he would smile and say, "Yep, I knew it, because I *saw* it!"

4. Persistence

Thomas Edison wrote, "Genius **is one percent inspiration**, ninety-nine percent perspiration." The Visionary Leader understands that maxim. Every great invention, event and entity was tried and re-tried and RE-TRIED until fruition.

The Visionary is committed to working hard and long hours to see his or her idea become realized. Like the Energizer Bunny there is no stopping for any reason. It's all or nothing. The reason for this is because the Visionary Leader does not work for someone, they work for a dream. Success or failure rests in his hands alone. There is no quit in his mind. Ever.

5. Resourceful

The most dynamic talent the Visionary Leader possesses is the means to accomplish anything in making the dream work. Because of his or her imagination, creativity, unlimited freedom, the ability to risk and nothing to lose, the ability to be resourceful is beyond powerful.

The average office worker or corporate executive is limited in many ways, but not the Visionary Leader. There is nothing to hold him back from solving any problem. Everything is available to him. If you give a visionary the freedom to work with an empty white board, you are giving him everything he needs to succeed. Just ask the Wright brothers, Vince Lombardi, or John F. Kennedy.

> **"Creativity requires the courage to let go of certainties."** Erich Fromm

The Visionary Leader is not concerned with security or safety when it comes to dreams and goals. It's about all-out passion and creativity to do what needs to be done.

There were over 400 of us sitting in the room that day awaiting the "big pitch" from our new CEO. It was our annual management meeting, a preparation for the next move on how to "win" against our competitors.

Our corporate color was green. We would joke that you would come out of those meetings so passionate for the cause, with great belief in our vision that if you were cut, you would bleed green.

This year was no exception.

The CEO proclaimed that even with the tremendous, record setting success we had achieved, the next 3 years would become our shining moment. He placed us on a call to become "Best in Class."

He compared us to organizations like IBM, Toyota, and Marriott. Yet we weren't a household name like they were. We were just a printing company that had nice growth.

Not anymore.

We were going to be the *best printing company* in the country. So much to the point that the number 1 printing company would want to join with us, not against us.

The vision had been set.

A key component in his message was the importance of effective teamwork. He played about 15 minutes from the movie *Apollo 13*.

Remember when all the engineers, technicians and operations team are trying to figure out how to get the broken ship back to earth? At first they fought, but once they worked together, magic happened. The vision was to take a ship with literally no power and bring it back home. To save the lives of the men on board.

They did it. And so did we.

Ever since that day, over 10 years ago, dreaming a vision into reality took on a new meaning for me. Visions are meant to be grand. Visions are meant to challenge practicality. Visions are meant to come true. Visions are wonderful things, along with those that dream them, they change the world.

"**Good business leaders create a vision, articulate the vision, passionately own the vision, and relentlessly drive it to completion.**" Jack Welch

Period.

End of story.

The Visionary Leader is a man or a woman who is interesting to be around, amazing in their imagination, and *a leader worth following*.

Stick around. This journey is going to blow your mind and broaden your world.

CHAPTER THREE

Appreciation: Lighting People Up!

**"Before you criticize people,
you should walk a mile in their shoes.
That way, when you criticize them...
you are a mile away from them...
and you have their shoes."** Jack Handey

A leader worth following must possess the ability to show appreciation to others. It not only helps define them, it changes the lives of the people they serve.

Appreciation: DEF. "An ability to understand the worth, quality or importance of something, an expression of admiration, approval, or gratitude."

People follow you because you make them feel wanted, needed and most of all, *valued.*

When you put their effort and energy on a mantel of honor they will respond in kind with even more energy.

Because you are *a leader worth following.*

My oldest son, Trevor, is in high school. He works at Chick-fil-A as a fry cook.

It's not rocket science but it's crucial to the operation of any fast food restaurant. Fries are a popular item. One night, his co-worker was sick and Trevor was left to handle the entire job alone.

Before long, the restaurant was packed with customers. Two lines formed and it was imperative that my son keep up with the demand to serve hundreds of customers. If not, it would be a disaster.

You do remember Lucy and Ethel frantically wrapping chocolates, right? Absolutely hilarious.

Trevor had to handle two lines at once, and did so without taking a break. To his credit, he never ran out of fries nor did anyone have to wait for their order during the four hours that defined his shift.

To say I was proud of my son is an understatement.

Someone else was proud of him, too. That individual told Trevor, "What you did with those fries was amazing!"

This praise did not come from a co-worker or a manager. They were words of appreciation from Beth, who had a major responsibility at that Chick-fil-A."

She was the owner.

My son was floating on air knowing he had impressed the boss. He felt appreciated by her compliment. Needless to say, he wanted to work even harder for her the next time.

I have been given thousands of dollars in bonuses and they do not have the IMPACT of one single compliment or an appreciative gesture.

It's even greater than the big check.

Think about it...once you spend the check, it's gone. The positive compliment from someone stays *forever*.

Appreciation.

It's the character quality that ignites a powerful potential in others and drives them to greatness.

It's a, "Surprise and Delight," style of leadership.

**"Show interest in all people,
not just those from whom you want something.
Making people feel important and good about
themselves is just the right thing to do."** Bo Bennett

Any successful organization understands this concept:

**"People treat others like
the leader treats them."**

As a leader you want the ultimate in customer service graciousness from your people.

It begins with *you*.

Express appreciation to those who work with customers.

Chick-fil-A is #1 in the quick-service chicken industry in the country, surpassing Popeye's, Church's, Zaxby's and KFC. This ranking is remarkable, considering they have 1/10th of the number of locations of their largest competitors. And, unlike their competitors, they are closed on Sundays.

What's their <u>secret</u>?

They know how to treat their employees and their customers. When you walk into one of their restaurants and say, "Thank you," they are trained to respond with, "My pleasure."

Appreciation is embedded deeply into their essence.

I used to work at a company, direct-mail kind of stuff. At times, one of the employees would fall behind on their machine. Instead of encouragement, my boss silently walked out on the floor and would turn up the machine to a *higher* level.

Then, with a frown at the employee, he would walk back to his office.

Two things happened as a result of his lack of appreciation here.

The employee would develop a bad attitude towards him and, as a result, would quietly turn down the pace of the machine, lower than it had been before.

My co-workers felt demeaned and demoralized. They didn't feel an iota of appreciation. It was a hostile work environment and it didn't need to be.

"Appreciation is when you publicly proclaim that someone else is valuable. So much so that the world needs to know that you believe it." Unknown

What are the *benefits* of showing appreciation to others?

There are several key ones here:

Personal Power

When people are appreciated it builds their self-confidence. It gives them a sense of validation that reminds them of their value. If someone goes through the day, or even a lifetime for that matter, without feeling appreciated it's a very lonely feeling. Empowerment, and believing in people, is a powerful weapon that produces great results through a loyalty to serve.

Motivation to work

When someone knows they are appreciated they want to live up to that truth by doing even more and doing it better than they ever did before. Need some proof. Think of a time when someone thanked you for the work you did, no matter how big or small. How did you feel about helping them the next time they asked?

Relationship

When you show your appreciation to someone you are deepening your bond with them. Remember, most people grow up with criticism so when you reach out positively to them it establishes a sense of connection between you both.

"Building great relationships is the key to building great companies."

Loyalty

Appreciating others deepens loyalty between the employer and employee. When you make someone smile they trust you more. When you make their day, they work to be more effective in their jobs.

Now, take that one step further. If employees have increased loyalty, strive to do great work, and serve your customers with a sense of appreciation and relationship building...you get a huge victory...

You increase the satisfaction of the customer. You broaden the customer experience and you deepen the engagement with your customer!

"Make it a habit to tell people thank you. Truly appreciate those around you, and you'll soon find many others around you. Truly appreciate life, and you'll find that you have more of it." Ralph Marston

Appreciation.

It has the power to boost a person's life as much as criticism does to betray it.

When I was in Little League I either walked or struck out every time. No matter how hard I tried, I couldn't hit the ball.

When I walked my coach would yell out to me as I trotted to first base, "Way to get a walk!"

It made me feel good.

Then, one day I struck out with the bat on my shoulder. My coach, normally an easy-going and gentle guy suddenly turned on me in front of everyone watching the game, "It's a sin to strike out without swinging!"

I was horrified.

Not only was he telling me I had made a baseball mistake but his reference rocked me to the depth of my soul.

A *sin*?

I was that bad?

Forgive me for being imperfect at the plate and for reacting to such a statement here but I had a good reason to be shell-shocked.

I was 8 years old.

"Appreciation is a wonderful thing: It makes what is excellent in others belong to us as well."
Voltaire

How much do you think I looked forward to my next trip to the plate?

Why are people unduly critical...why is it difficult for them to praise you?

A few thoughts:

Human nature

It is normal for humans to think the worst, rather than the best, of situations and people. People tend to live with fear and foreboding based on a negative nature rather than on a positive plane. Hence, it is easier for them to point out your faults.

Self-success jealousy

A lot of people are competitive. Sometimes, they don't appreciate someone becoming more successful than them. It makes them crazy. If they can limit you or put you down, in their minds it makes them better than you.

Our culture

When you turn on the news at night what do you usually see? You watch people doing *bad* things, not good ones. It is not newsworthy to give us positive events. When you consider that most Americans watched hundreds of thousands of hours of news reporting in their lifetime, do the math.

Selfish

People get absorbed in their work, their lives and what is important to them. Too many so called "leaders" today just expect results. They are in a word, selfish.

In summary, choose to be a person who appreciates others. Make it one of your mantras. A leader who knows how to point out the good things someone does will always be one worth following.

Not only will you inspire loyalty in your troops, you will engender love in the world. That will make them a better person...and someone else as well.

You.

Remember that appreciation can come in the form of a small act. Something simple, yet from the heart. It can be big and grand, yet most importantly, it needs to express gratitude for *who* the person is and what they *mean* to you, and if applicable, to your organization.

Many years ago, an associate and I were tasked by our companies' leadership to improve the sales of the organization. Our Senior VP truly appreciated our ideas, our work, and our friendship. He valued us as people and was thankful for being able to work with us each day.

Yes, getting results mattered. However, there was a higher sense of gratitude toward us for our passion to serve the clients, the team and the vision.

We didn't make our goals that first year, yet, he knew the work would pay off in time. He also wanted to say "thank you" to us, to express his appreciation, to build loyalty, to reinforce that good things happen to good people.

There were no bonus payouts that year, for anyone. There were only very small salary increases. Times were tough, the economy was sluggish and hurting companies everywhere. Including ours.

Yet, with all that said, great leaders find ways to appreciate those that are important in their lives. He did just that for the two of us that year.

We were just a few weeks from a scheduled business trip to attend an industry conference in February. The location was near the ocean in Florida.

Reminder, I lived near Chicago, Illinois.

He called my close business associate and I into his office and closed the door. He shared with us how much he and the company appreciated us, our work ethic, our vision, and they wanted to say "thank you" in a special way.

They treated us to a little "business getaway."

They paid for our wives to join us on our business trip, to spend our free moments enjoying time with them, taking them out for dinner and simply re-energizing during our trip. What would have been a typical conference turned into a memorable and special couples trip. We had a blast.

The extra airfare expenses for our wives and picking up a few meals didn't really cost our company very much money at all. Yet, the total value of their appreciation to us?

Priceless.

We knew that no matter how hard things may get, no matter how frustrating the challenges might be, we were a part of something special. We worked for leaders that truly knew what mattered. They cared for us as people.

They found a simple way to appreciate us.

Our loyalty to them as people, and as a company, would never be stronger.

They didn't do it for the ROI. They did it because they wanted to.

Yet, the ROI was terrific. Their act of appreciation fueled the fire within us to treat our employees and our clients in the same manner.

Over the next five years we grew sales and profits of our 65 year-old company by over 50%.

I look back at his gesture, at the memories we made on that trip, the time I shared with my wife and my friend, and I am forever grateful for the generosity of my manager and the company.

I love my wife, and I love spending time with her. The ability to bring her into my working life on that trip changed my perspective on business travel, forever. Ever since then, I ask her to join me whenever she can.

I will always be thankful for those that have shown appreciation to me and do my best to show that same appreciation to others.

"Spend time with a person you love the most, the one you care for. Make them feel special, for you never know when time will take them away from you forever!" William Swanson

Appreciate others.

Make their day.

They will follow you forever.

CHAPTER FOUR

Character-Driven Success

"The end doesn't always justify the means but character always does." William Hansell

The most infamous marathon runner in history was a lady named Rosie Ruiz. Originally from Cuba, Ruiz ran in the legendary Boston Marathon in 1980. She not only ran in the race, she recorded the fastest time of any female in the history of the Boston Marathon and the third fastest time for a woman in marathon history.

There was a good reason for her high level of running success.

She cheated.

When she hit the finish line she wasn't coated in perspiration nor was she even out of breath. Rather than wrapping up a 26 mile run she looked like she had spent the last two hours at high tea at a five-star hotel.

Her winning time was almost a half an hour *faster* than her previous marathon race in New York City six months earlier. She also had flabby thighs belying the physical legs of a champion long-distance runner.

She did not appear in any video footage of the race, and she was seen by two students from Harvard University emerging suddenly from a crowd of spectators not far from the finish line.

Rosie Ruiz was not a champion, she was a con artist. She was disqualified by the Boston Marathon officials. To this day, Ruiz claims to have won the race fairly.

Her "performance" is a classic example of, "The ends justifies the means." Many people in corporate America believe that, "succeeding at all costs is acceptable."

But, the Leader Worth Following has a different take on that maxim, "Only **character counts** when it comes to the ultimate success."

If you win or succeed unfairly, that isn't a victory at all. At least not one in which your conscience will join you at the finish line unless you are a sociopath or a pathological liar.

 "If I take care of my character, my success will take care of itself." Thomas Fenton

There is a bottom line to the bottom line here.

There is principal and then there is **principle**.

Principal is financial profit and principle is the moral measurement. *Principle* is the step hundreds of companies and thousands of executives fail to add to their standard of success.

It is vital to set that core foundation if a business is going to thrive in the long run. Companies such as Wal-Mart, Chick-fil-A, Target, Microsoft, JCPenny, Costco,

Home Depot, Google and Intel are all known for their generous donations and commitment to taking care of their employees over profits.

These corporations don't believe that, "the end justifies the means." They believe there is a qualifier in that phrase which should be focused on the quality of the means to reach the ultimate goal.

Perfect examples of character-driven companies.

As a result, they make a lot of money along the way.

Win – Win.

A prime example of this is found in the person of NBA Hall of Famer, Larry Bird. On the day he informed the management of the Boston Celtics he was retiring the President of the team, Red Auerbach, met with Larry and offered him a multi-million dollar salary to play one more year in 1993.

Bird turned it down.

Auerbach was shocked. He told his legendary player, "I know you have a bad back but I'm not concerned about that. Just stay on the team and collect your final year of salary. You've earned it."

His player was having none of it, "If I can't play to the best of my ability for the team, I'm not taking the money."

After arguing for several minutes, Bird won out.

He retired as a player and gave up millions of dollars in doing so. His personal character and integrity were more important to him than the easy money he could have drawn here.

"It is not by muscle, speed, or physical dexterity that great things are achieved, but by reflection, force of character, and judgment." Cicero

Larry Bird was a great player but more importantly he is a great *man.*

If more leaders had the same attitude as Larry Bird our country would thrive in principal and principle. It's that character-driven success that needs to be front and center in the hearts of individuals and at the foundation of corporations.

This foundation seemed to elude Michael Madoff, Dennis Kozlowski and Bernie Madoff, among other unscrupulous executives, who allowed greed to pervade their conscience, their soul and ultimately their professional companies.

The question before you is powerful,

"When it comes to your career what is your goal?"

If your goal is status and material success, then your means of getting there may not be founded in integrity but in success at all costs. You might achieve all your dreams and lose your soul in the process.

Set your goal based upon character, *now*, to ensure your success both in the public and personal workplace of your being. If you are young and starting out, this is the perfect time to align your moral compass.

If you are in mid-career and need a course adjustment, do it today. The sooner and the more committed you are to instill integrity in your soul will determine the ultimate end goal of your success and fulfillment.

"A man's character is his fate." Heraclitus

How can you jump start a career of conscience?

Here's a list for those who want to pursue a character-driven success in life:

1. **A commitment to honesty**

   Make a promise to yourself that from this point on you will always tell the truth in any, and every, situation. In doing so, you will never have to worry about compromising yourself or your business decisions.

2. **Negotiable and non-negotiable**

   Money, profits and material success are negotiable. Character, integrity and honesty are non-negotiable. So, whenever you have a conflict between the two entities, your decision should always be to choose the *non-negotiable* option.

3. **Immerse yourself in character, not characters**

   In your lifetime, you will be meeting individuals who are colorful, fast-talking, shrewd, opportunistic and full of self-serving ideas. They are called *characters*. But, do not allow yourself to give them power over you. Choose men and women of *characters*, including a personal and professional mentor, to be that safe fence of integrity protecting you from moral harm. You will never regret it.

4. People first

When you make a decision, always put the interests of the people you serve ahead of your own ambitions. Take care of your people and create opportunities for their success.

5. Good money and bad money

This is simple. Any ill-gotten financial gain is bad money. Any profits you engender out of character and integrity is good money. Spend your life pursuing the financial gains of good money based on your conscience, your moral values and your desire to help others flourish because of it.

You will never regret it.

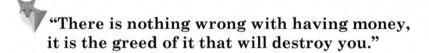 **"There is nothing wrong with having money, it is the greed of it that will destroy you."**

Life is full of choices. In every moment, we have options. There are different directions our *journey to success* can take us.

The question is, when everything is on the line, which choice will you make? And by everything, I don't mean millions of dollars, or your career. I mean your character.

I was out to eat at a national fast casual restaurant and when the bill arrived, I realized it was incorrect. We had been overcharged. I asked them to take the charges off my bill and I would be happy to pay what I owe.

They did, and so did I.

Simple.

I am sure you, like most people, would stand up to *not* pay for anything you didn't owe.

One Christmas vacation my family and I were enjoying our Christmas Eve dinner sitting at an outdoor restaurant in Southern California.

It was terrific.

We weren't freezing from the Midwest winter or fighting traffic in the Chicago suburbs, we were sitting in an uncrowded area soaking up the fresh air, the great food and friendly service. It was a wonderful evening with my wife and children.

After our evening was complete, the bill came. I placed my credit card in the holder and our server returned with the receipts, a beautiful smile and Christmas wishes. As I signed the bill, it came to my attention that it might be incorrect. I paused, looked at the itemized listing and realized that we were not charged enough. The total should have been at least $20 more than what we were paying.

My family had already made their way out to the car, so I paused by the front desk. Our server came running in my direction, and here is how the conversation went with her, we will call her Sarah:

Sarah: Oh, sir, is there something wrong, did I make a mistake?

Me: Actually, yes. It seems that you didn't charge us for two items, our bill should be higher.

Sarah: I am so sorry. Let me see.....oh, just don't worry about it.

Me: Well, you don't have to do that, I owe more and am happy to pay for my share.

Sarah: It was my mistake, please accept it as our gift, Merry Christmas!

Me: Merry Christmas to you, and thank you!

When it comes to integrity, she revealed to me how powerful it can be. I hope that every person that is charged more than they should be would do the same. Even in the little things, our character matters.

Schools have character counts programs for good reason. They are teaching our children that trustworthiness and fairness matters. The language talks about how stealing, cheating and not playing by the rules will hurt you.

Question for you, is there any difference in cheating on a test in school and lying about the age of your child to get a discount at a retailer or at the movies?

Is there a difference between *knowing* that I got away with paying just $20 less than I should have and hiding $20,000 from my clients in fraudulent billing charges?

Character is more than just a fancy program name, it is the cement that your road to success is built on. For that road to be long and prosperous, you need it to be built with strength of integrity, honor and truth. Remember this:

**"All roads lead somewhere,
it just depends upon where
you want to end up."** Unknown

Always make it your mission to be a person of *character-driven success.*

That is how you live out this wisdom straight from my grandfather:

"You need to like the person you see in the mirror each morning."

Do that, and you will be *a leader worth following.*

CHAPTER FIVE

Be the Leader *and* the Follower

As a Chicago native I struggle to admit, but Aaron Rodgers will be a Hall of Fame inductee. He is a record setting NFL quarterback and a Super Bowl MVP. He is also one of the most famous *followers* in sports history.

He became great by sitting down and watching two geniuses teach him how to excel at the game. The leaders that he followed were Mike McCarthy, the veteran coach, and the starting quarterback who overshadowed him, Green Bay's beloved two time Super Bowl champion, Brett Favre.

In 2007-2008, Rodgers sat on the bench and watched the legendary Favre set one record after another. Most wins by a quarterback, most touchdown passes by a quarterback and yet another Pro Bowl after he became only the third quarterback in history to defeat all 31 teams. Brett got all the glory but Aaron was quietly picking up vital information on how to be the ultimate NFL winner.

Finally, in 2008, with Favre retired/traded (that is a different story) Aaron Rodgers got his chance to be the starting signal caller.

In his first season at the helm, Rodgers threw for over 4,000 yards and 28 touchdowns. A terrific start, but he was just getting warmed up.

In 2010, he led the Packers to the Super Bowl and a 31−25 victory over Pittsburgh. He most deservedly was the MVP of that championship with his 304 passing yards, 3 touchdown passes and no interceptions.

In 2011, he had one of the greatest seasons in NFL history. He threw for 4,643 passing yards, 45 touchdown passes, and only six interceptions, good for a passer rating of 122.5, which is currently the highest single season passer rating in NFL history.

Aaron has the highest touchdown to interception ratio in NFL history at 4.0, nearly doubling the closest competitor. His overall career passer rating is 106.5, highest ever in the NFL. Rodgers' also holds the record for highest passer rating in a season and for the most consecutive seasons of 100+ ratings. He holds the record for most passing yards in the first 5 years as a starter with 21,332...and the list goes on.

Not bad for a *follower,* huh?

Great leaders are also great followers.

Exhibit A: Aaron Rodgers

"Your time has come to shine, all your dreams are on their way." Simon & Garfunkel, *Bridge Over Troubled Waters*

Thousands of great leaders had to wait their turn and learn from the leaders that preceded them. This was not a humiliating experience for them but a *humbling* one. It educated them on how to refine their talents for the moment they would be taking over the helm and it taught them patience and depth of experience.

When their time came to be in the spotlight, they were ready to shine.

One of my favorite long time co-workers is Jeannette Duncan. We met early in our careers, we were just out of college. We worked together for about a year at the same location and became good friends. I truly enjoyed working with her.

Like many young twenty-somethings, we loved to work and play hard. We were sponges when it came to learning and advancing in our careers, too. We had everything before us. Life was terrific.

Our positions and pathways to promotion were a bit different, yet we were both placed in "the fast track" program. We were called "plant manager trainees."

This process placed us in a long term development program that would ultimately put us as potential plant managers within 5–7 years. We would have to hold a variety of positions, and potentially relocate every year or two.

We would work with the best leaders in our company. We would be trained in multiple disciplines from operations to sales, to finance, estimating and customer service. It was a terrific training and mentoring experience.

The commitment was huge; so was the opportunity.

A few years into our program, after several job changes and relocations, I was moved and promoted to the Assistant Plant Manager of one of our largest production plants. Upon receiving my assignment, I was pleasantly surprised to find the customer service manager was, of course, Jeannette.

We would be back together again!

This time, she would actually report to me. The two of us had been in waiting for the big role and I was on my next to last stop.

Even though I was now in line "ahead" of Jeannette for future promotions, there was no resentment. We were a great team. I invested a lot of my time working with Jeannette. She was a promising leader and I did my best in helping her continue to grow.

The plant manager I worked with (and under) was just a year older than me, yet he was one of the best. They placed me there because they had a need I could fill, and they knew I would get terrific training, which is exactly what happened.

Keith put finishing touches on my leadership and financial decision making skills that gave me what I needed to become a plant manager. In just 15 short months, I was promoted.

My 5 year journey had come to an end. I now had my own plant to lead. Finally, after sitting in waiting, learning, watching, failing, improving...I have reached a major leadership pinnacle.

Within a year of my new tenure as the Plant Manager of the $30 million operation, I needed a "right hand" manager. The call went to Jeannette. We worked together in that facility for over 4 years and were very successful. We launched new products, grew the business and of course, I invested in leading Jeannette.

I made a major switch and moved to a small, privately held, company as their Vice President of Operations. Within a year I needed a new Operations Manager.

Any guesses to what I did?

Of course, I made one phone call and Jeannette came on board.

That role fit her professional and personal needs and life goals perfectly. Nearly 10 years later, she still holds that position and loves it. I am honored to have been one that helped her accomplish so much.

Remember this:

"The person that is both a follower and a leader is part of a powerful chain that sustains greatness in our world."

As you prepare for your moments of triumph, here are suggestions for you to be ready to step up when the call is made to stand tall as a leader of others.

Don't be jealous of your leader, embrace their leadership

The better follower you are the better *leader* you will be. Praise those ahead of you, pick their brain and always promote their talents to others. They have earned their status as the leader and you need to honor that about them. Your day to lead will come, for now, be the supportive follower.

Do your homework, know your stuff as well as the leader

When the executives are ready to promote you to leadership, you need to be worthy of it. That takes one word, *preparation.* Noah built the ark before the rains came. He was ready. Stop worrying about *when* you will get the call. Instead, put your energy into *what* you will do *when* you are promoted. Remain positive and proactive.

"Failure to prepare is preparing to fail." Mike Murdock

Don't gossip or undermine them

Being critical of the man or woman in the position you are seeking will make you look petty and jealous. If you get that reputation you will never be promoted to any leadership position. They are watching you to see if you will be a team player and someone who can be entrusted to lead others.

Go out of your way to learn everything you can from them

Be a <u>know-nothing</u> and let them pour their knowledge and experience into you instead of being a <u>know-it-all</u> who believes you are the expert. Here's a clue, even if you are an expert, acting like one will convince the powers-that-be you're <u>*not*</u>!

Stay humble with a servant-like attitude

Treat the leader above you the same way you would want your followers to admire you. Be a follower with character if you want your followers to look up to you.

**"Do you wish to rise? Begin by descending.
You plan a tower that will pierce the clouds?
Lay first the foundation of humility."** Saint Augustine

I have a friend named PJ. All his growing up life he functioned as a follower. In the 4th grade he ran for President of his class and lost. In 5th grade he tried out for the basketball team and never got to play but he won the, "Sportsmanship Award."

In 7th grade he went out for the Pop Warner football team and wound up as the water boy serving others. As a freshman in high school he ran for student rep for his class and lost. He ran for the treasurer of the Student Body at sixteen and lost. He tried out for the high school basketball team that same year and was cut from the team.

PJ ran for President in his senior year and lost *again.* As a freshman in college he ran for student body representative and was defeated and in his junior year he ran for student senate and...guess what?

He lost again!

But, in all those situations he was never a sore loser. He was a gracious winner. He worked hard to support every person who had beaten him and this ability to follow paid off in dividends as an adult.

PJ became a very successful man. He played multiple sports in college and was named All-Conference in basketball. He is a leader in education, television and the publishing industry. He has won more awards and honors than most people in the United States.

Why?

Because he learned the art of following and it served as his foundation for leadership.

Instead of becoming bitter or disheartened, he saw every attempt he made as a successful learning experience. It strengthened his resolve and it gave him the ability to succeed beyond the people who had never lost.

**"Remember the two benefits of failure.
First, if you do fail, you learn what doesn't work;
and second, the failure gives you
the opportunity to try a new approach."** Roger von Oech

I think PJ views himself as I see myself...never as a failure...only a success *waiting* to happen!

Learn to be a great follower and you will in turn be a great leader.

A leader worth following.

CHAPTER SIX

Personal Responsibility

The most popular sport in America is not football or baseball, the most favored recreational activity among millions of us is *The Blame Game.*

We play it passionately and for the purpose of always making ourselves look good no matter who else it hurts in the process. It's not played with a ball or a bat but its final score always hurts someone, either the person we are blaming, or ourselves.

"If you could kick the person in the pants responsible for most of your trouble, you wouldn't sit for a month." Theodore Roosevelt

A leader worth following is not an athlete in the blame game. He or she does not focus on the faults of others. He sits that game out. He chooses to live or die with his own actions.

In 1945, the United States was part of the Allied Forces in World War II. We had stopped Adolph Hitler in Europe and had brought them to a formal surrender in May of that year.

However, our enemy to the east, Japan, was dug in and unwilling to stop fighting. The Empire of the Sun had amassed over two million soldiers to protect their borders and they were prepared to wage war against us indefinitely.

Our President, Harry S. Truman, was advised that a prolonged conflict with the Japanese could result in the combined deaths of a million more lives unless we made a strong and decisive move to end the war with a very stubborn and passionate foe.

On August 6, 1945, Truman authorized such a move.

The United States dropped an atomic bomb on the Japanese city of Hiroshima killing over 70,000 citizens instantly. On August 9, we did it again. This time the target was Nagasaki and 80,000 Japanese were instantly vaporized.

On August 14, Japan surrendered. The war was abruptly over.

A firestorm of criticism ensued with President Truman in the cross hairs of the outcry. No country, before or since, had ever used a nuclear weapon on another nation.

Was it ethical?

Was it humane?

The President of the United States explained his reasoning. Instead of blaming his Joint Chiefs of Staff, his military advisors, or other countries in the Allied Forces, he took *full* responsibility for his decision.

In one of the most phrases ever that defined a leader's philosophy, Harry Truman later had a little sign on his desk,

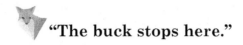 **"The buck stops here."**

His challenge to us is clear.

It starts and ends with you.

Fateful choices in history made by men and women stopped and ended with their decision to do what they had to do, even if it cost them their lives. A few are worth noting here,

"Give me liberty or give me death!"

This capped a great challenge by Patrick Henry, one of our most famous patriots in the Revolutionary War to the Virginia House of Burgesses, to authorize troops from Virginia to stand up to King George III and the British army and become independent as a new nation.

Thomas Marshall, who was in the audience, told his son, John Marshall, (who later became the most revered Chief Justice of the Supreme Court in American history), that the speech was "one of the most bold, vehement, and animated pieces of eloquence that had ever been delivered."

"Remember the Alamo!"

Davy Crockett took that responsibility to heart and it cost him his life. He was not alone. The leader of that Spanish mission was Colonel William Travis and he gave his men, 182 in all, three choices: Rush the enemy, the massive Mexican army advancing to the small fortress to kill all of them; surrender, which would result in their execution or remain and defend it to the last man.

In all three cases, they would die. The fourth option was to sneak out and flee and it was a viable choice but not one man took it.

In the end, there were no survivors inside that mission. But, the bravery they exhibited and the personal responsibility they chose made each of them *a leader worth following*. It also led to Texas becoming our 28th state in 1845.

> **"My fellow Americans, ask not what**
> **your country can do for you,**
> **ask what you can do for your country."**

In his inaugural address on the first day of his Presidency, John F. Kennedy put personal responsibility to the national and social test. Heralding an attitude that all Americans needed to hear, he clearly spelled out we, as citizens, should be unselfish and focused on matters outside ourselves.

Today, in the world of social networking, egoism and selfies, this famous line seems more like a novelty of the past instead of a valid challenge to the heart of every American.

> **"I only regret that I have but one life**
> **to give for my country."** Nathan Hale

His statement is the heart of personal responsibility. Nathan Hale uttered these words before he was executed for spying on the British in the Revolutionary War. He stood by his actions without making excuses. He did not point fingers at any of the soldiers at his side.

This is a man who passionately stood for liberty without regret and will always be remembered as a true patriot and leader of our nation's heritage.

"I will not surrender responsibility for my life and my actions." John Enoch Powell

A leader worth following understands the depth and power of making and sticking to his or her own decisions. They cannot be carried by the drifts of wind, by the popular politics of the day or the prevailing views of the masses.

They have to be fiercely tied to their conscience and the value system that emanates from it.

Being a true advocate of *personal responsibility* requires a rock-solid foundation without compromise even for those moments of temptation and weakness that may buckle our moral knees at times.

Here are 10 keys to personal accountability:

1. **Understand the difference between convictions and beliefs**

   Most of us grow up on the borrowed beliefs of our parents and their views on life. This isn't good enough for us. We need to develop real *convictions* about what we believe in our own souls.

   Until we do, it will be difficult for any of us to really trust our personal responsibility in every situation.

It cannot come from our parental guideline. It must come from *within* us. That's more than a family belief that is a foundational rock we can always stand on.

2. The big 3

There are three attitudes you need to dismantle in order to practice personal responsibility as a way of life. They are making excuses, bitterness, and finding fault in the performances of those around you. These attitudes are like pervasive weeds. If they have a stranglehold on you there will be no chance for personal responsibility to ever take root.

3. Consider *your* responsibility in a blaming situation

As the noted attorney Louis Nizer, was fond of saying, "When a man points a finger at someone else, he should remember that four of his fingers are pointing at himself."

Hold up your hand and form it into a gun and you will get the point. Now, stop pointing out the faults of others. You are only shooting yourself.

4. Realize the value of your life's uniqueness

If you truly respect yourself as being one of a kind, then your approach to responsibility should always reflect that belief. A unique individual doesn't spend his time worrying about other people and what they did or said to make a situation go bad.

He or she should focus on the personal aspect of how they should have made the problem solvable.

5. Do what *you* do well

Personal responsibility means just that, personal. When you focus on others and their successes or failures you lose sight of your own performance. Vince Lombardi always instilled in his players, "It doesn't matter what the other team is doing, it only matters what *we* do."

That's why his Green Bay Packers were legendary. It mattered very little what defense the other team played or how effective their own offense could be. The Pack rolled them at will. Pay attention to what *you* need to do and do it well. Always.

6. Individuality not image

Everyone is insecure about something. Everyone fails several times per day at some level. This should tell you that you should never worry about your image being better or worse than the next person. Just be yourself and let other insecure people worry about their image.

When you find joy and personal power in who you are, it will result in only one expression of life, a habit of ongoing personal responsibility.

7. The blame game trap

Somehow, we get it into our minds that tearing others down or blaming them makes *us* better. It doesn't. Success is determined by *our* performance, not on the mistakes of others.

Until we realize that our real value is in ourselves and in our work, we will be petty and critical of everyone around us. Don't fall into that trap. It's what *you do* that defines your value.

8. Study the historical greatness of personal responsibility

Inundate yourself with the heroic men and women of America who took a personal stand for justice and truth at the cost of their own success or reputation. This will empower you to follow their example and make it your own.

9. Always tell the truth

President Nixon gave us all a classic demonstration of failure to accept personal responsibility. How? He lied. When you lie you are always attempting to deflect the focus off yourself. It not only cost him his Presidency, it cost him his reputation. Never let that happen to you. Whenever faced with the decision to tell the truth or be dishonest, take the high road. It may not be the best short-term solution but in the long run it is the greatest thing you will ever do.

10. Live for something that is worth dying for

Being *a leader worth following* is not a convenient political ploy for personal gain. It requires living with moral convictions, like honesty, integrity, character, humility and a foundation of personal responsibility.

Only a man or woman who is living a life that is worth dying for will exhibit those qualities over the course of their existence. The reason so many leaders fall into scandal is because they don't value their ethical contribution to the people around them.

My story on taking personal responsibility:

A friend of mine asked if I was interested in helping him with some real estate dealings. He was looking for people that wanted to buy a home on a rent-to-own contract. It was early in the 2000's and the market was booming!

I was intrigued.

My role would be simple. Find people for the homes.

Easy.

And it was.

We did very well in placing families in the homes. The business grew. Well, his business grew.

I became interested in wanting more, a bigger piece of the action. He became tapped from a leverage perspective and could no longer secure loans to buy homes. So, he turned to me.

There was a willing family and a home to buy in Ohio. I lived in Illinois, but no worries, I was in! Within a few months I owned two homes, so exciting!

I was in the real estate investment business.

What I failed to recognize were all the downsides and parts of the business that aren't so wonderful.

Things like repairs. Tenants that damage homes. Tenants that don't pay on time, or at all. Did I mention repairs? Tenants that move out, and then no one moves in for months on end. The list goes on.

And then it happened...2008.

The market crashed.

Repairs mounted. The market rate for rent lowered by 25% and the value of the homes dropped over 50%.

Like many people, we owed more on the homes than they were worth.

There was a time that one home sat vacant for nearly 1 ½ years.

No income. Just bills.

To say this was a financial burden on my family is an understatement.

As I shared my story with people, many of them encouraged me to do one of two things. Either, short sale the home, or just walk away.

I was puzzled. Walk away?

"Everyone is doing it." Some would say to me. "You are losing tens of thousands of dollars, you don't want that, just walk away."

Then I would hear a whisper from my past. My grandfather's voice would speak to me. I could hear him saying:

 "Keep your name and your credit good, it will beat you to the next place."

There it was. Wisdom for the ages.

Take responsibility for your actions.

Don't blame others. Keep your word, pay your debts. You decided to play…now you have to pay.

I had signed an obligation to pay those loans.
I had decided to buy the homes and enter the business.
I needed, and would, take responsibility for my decisions.

That *friend* I mentioned at the beginning of this story didn't fair so well. He decided to escape. He bailed on everything. He filed for bankruptcy. He divorced his wife and left his kids. He chose to destroy everything of *real* importance in order to save some money.

That is NOT *a leader worth following.*

I still own the homes today. I have good families in them. The business investment may not have gone as planned, but my credit is great.

I honored my word. I can look myself in the mirror each morning knowing that I took personal responsibility for my actions. I did what was right because it was the right thing to do.

Your life is in your hands. It's up to you.

**"Have the courage to say no.
Have the courage to face the truth.
Do the right thing because it is right."**
W. Clement Stone

CHAPTER SEVEN

Leave a Legacy

How will people remember you when you depart from this earth?

When your name is mentioned what will be the first thing they will think of…an inventor who made the world better, a person who discovered a cure for a deadly disease, a gifted athlete who died too soon, someone who lived by inspirational quotations or a famous celebrity beloved by the world?

What others will think of you will be your legacy.

It matters not how many good or bad things you did in your lifetime because in the end it is what is finally attached to your name that will be what you accomplished in the eyes of history.

Richard Nixon had a remarkable political career. His presidency opened doors for our country to Russia and China. He ended the war in Vietnam. He could have been one of the great political leaders of the 20th Century.

But, his legacy will always be linked to *Watergate*. He is remembered by one word: *Liar*.

Elvis was the King of Rock and Roll. His music will live on in the hearts of millions forever. He was beyond handsome, charismatic and talented. But, at the end, too many people will think of one word related to Elvis Presley when his name is mentioned: *Drugs.*

OJ Simpson was one of the greatest running backs in college and pro football history. His ability to carry the football was rivaled only by Jim Brown, Walter Payton and Gale Sayers. He was a champion on the field, but he will never be remembered for winning the Heisman Trophy. His legacy is set in eternal stone: *Criminal.*

The list goes on and on like a permanent word association game…Edison/inventor, Salk/polio, da Vinci/Mona Lisa, Pete Rose/gambler, Enron/scandal, LBJ/Vietnam War, Robert Kennedy/assassinated, Davy Crockett/Alamo, and so on.

Our legacy.

Good or bad, that is the way it was, is, and always will be.

What will be *yours?*

"When it's all over, it's not who you were… it's whether you made a difference." Bob Dole

Throughout history there have been thousands of notable men and women who have left exemplary legacies that are familiar to us, from George Washington to Clara Barton to Eleanor Roosevelt and Ronald Reagan. These are the famous people we all know about.

In highlighting what it means to leave a legacy, let's focus on an average guy who left his forever mark during one of the most tragic events in our nation's history.

His name was Dave Sanders.

The tragic event was at Columbine High School.

April 20, 1999.

Sanders had already established a credible legacy as a teacher and a father of three girls. He was a hero to his daughters and to all the students in his class. Had he died before April 20, he would have been remembered fondly for his sacrifice, love, and commitment to those he served in a small, but meaningful way.

When two sadistic teenage killers entered the high school that fateful morning, Dave Sanders established a far greater legacy than even he could ever imagine.

Before we discuss what he did, let's state what he didn't do.

When the shots first rang out, most of the teachers in the school left the building immediately and fled to safety. This would be an understandable action. Gunshots usually bring wounds and death.

Not David Sanders. He ran in the opposite direction of safety. He ran *toward* the gunshots.

Legacy.

"The choices we make about the lives we live determine the kinds of legacies we leave." Tavis Smiley

Instead of joining his co-educators in the parking lot, far from any danger, Dave Sanders plunged right into the middle of it. He evacuated the cafeteria, pushing hundreds of students out just before the student killers entered the room.

It was an amazing act of heroism, courage and sacrifice. It cost him his life.

As the last person to flee, Sanders was hit twice with bullets and collapsed in a nearby classroom where some students had barricaded themselves inside. As he lay dying he said, "Let me see my girls." They pulled the photograph from his wallet and showed him his three young daughters.

It was one of the last things Dave Sanders would ever see. He died on the way to the hospital, the only teacher at Columbine to be murdered that day.

He, of course, will be remembered as a daddy, teacher and coach.

Yet, even greater than all those wonderful legacies, he will leave the ultimate legacy; giving his life for others. The greatest act of selflessness imaginable.

**"No one shows greater love
than when he lays down his life for his friends."**
John 15:13

David Sanders, a very common man, has an eternal legacy attached to his name that is extraordinary. His daughters will be proud of him every day of their lives.

Legacies come in all shapes, sizes and textures. No two are the same, just like human beings. But, everyone of us will be attached to one, like it or not. People will remember us for *something*.

Here are some of the categories that may suit your final contribution to the life you led from birth to death.

What you may leave behind:

Your heirs

The family legacy: your son, daughter or grandchildren carrying on your dreams, business, passions and worldwide influence.

For me, it's my grandfather to my mother, and then to my brother and me. We now leave a legacy to our children, in total, there are six. How they and their grandchildren will go on to change the world is yet to be decided.

Whatever happens, it is part of my family legacy.

Your business

A family-owned business can go on for hundreds of years serving local communities. Wal-Mart, J.C. Penney, McDonald's, Marriott, Hilton and Disney are big names that come to mind here. Other great generational work related legacies include Billy and Franklin Graham as they evangelize to the world.

Think of the tens of thousands of local stores, farms and small town businesses that carry a family name on the sign, and are being run by the great grandchildren.

"My work...is my legacy." Patrick Swayze

Your followers

As a teacher, a preacher, a pastor, a coach or a mentor, your legacy is the success of those you influence. Whether in the classroom, the boardroom, the locker room or the family room, you have influenced generations long after you passed away. They will carry the torch of your influence, ideas and inspiration wherever they go.

"The key to successful leadership today is influence not authority." Ken Blanchard

Your inventions

People will remember the legacies of Alexander Graham Bell, the Wright Brothers, Nikola Tesla, Henry Ford, Bill Gates and Thomas Edison until the end of the world. We owe them all a great deal of gratitude. They have changed the world forever.

Your inspirational writings and oratory

Nothing survives like the written and spoken word in people's lives, forever. Once someone reads something or hears something that motivates them it is locked into their soul and it enriches their every day lives.

If you are a word smith or a gifted speaker, your legacy will most likely come in one of these areas of remembrance.

Your passions

Great leaders and influential people work from their soul to make the world a better place. Often times, their passion lives on even after they die. William Holden fought for the wild animals surviving in Kenya, Princess Diana was consumed with making the world safe from land mines and Angelina Jolie and Brad Pitt spent thousands of hours ministering to the less fortunate in Third-World countries.

What *passionate* cause do you want to see carried on beyond your life?

Your charitable giving

Robin Williams was a gifted comedian and actor. He was also one of the most generous individuals on the planet. He donated and raised hundreds of millions of dollars with charities like, *Comic Relief* to make the world a better place.

Bill Gates, Paul Allen, George Soros and Michael Bloomberg head the list of those who gave away millions of dollars for the relief of the suffering in the world. God Bless them!

Your love

The first name that comes to mind here is Mother Teresa of Calcutta. She was a humble woman but one of the kindest and most loving souls on earth. She made the world a better place simply by giving her heart away.

How can you love someone in a way they will never forget? How can you love someone that helps them love others? The contagion of love is powerful and one of the strongest legacies you can leave.

Your character

Never underestimate ethics and integrity as a legacy of your life. They are not only marks of *a leader worth following,* they are essentials to the well-being and conscience of the world.

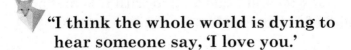 **"I think the whole world is dying to hear someone say, 'I love you.'**

**I think that if I can leave the legacy of love
and passion in the world, then I think
I've done my job in a world that's getting
colder and colder by the day."** Lionel Richie

Legacies are as important as the life lived supporting them.

This book has been a dedication to leaders with character, integrity, and a heart to make the world a better place because they were in it.

As I have mentioned, my grandfather was one of those men in my life.

I remember the many stories, teaching moments, one-liners and wisdom he shared and instilled in my life. None, however, stands more prominent then our moments together on December 27, 1998.

I remember the day well, because it was the last day I saw him.

It was the last time we spoke.

He was dying from cancer.

He was too weak to eat much, too weak to leave his home, and too weak to be part of the family Christmas celebration.

My wife and I had visited with him and my grandma for about an hour.

It was very special.

We had our one year old son with us, the first great-grand child in the family.

My grandpa held my son, and it was all I could do to hold back the tears.

I knew this moment would never be replicated.

I quickly took a picture, which still sits in my kitchen to this day.

Our talk moved from the weather, to our family, to what we were doing at home, to my job.

I was the assistant plant manager for a billion dollar company. We had over 250 employees. It was a 24 hour, 7 day a week production operation. It was a big deal in the corporate world.

With all that said, he wanted to talk about my family.

As we left, we hugged and said our final goodbye. Just as I was about to leave, he had one, final message for me.

This was his legacy moment, his final words to me...

What would he say?

Would it be about how to climb the ladder? Or, maybe, something funny to lighten up the moment? Maybe he would give me the short cut to having a great life as he did...you know, "making it."

He put his hand firmly on my shoulder. He looked deeply in my eyes and said:

"Take care of your family, kid!"

That was it.

Of all the leadership wisdom he had shared with me, of all the topics he could have chosen, this was his finest moment.

His legacy was clear.

Nothing is more important than your family.

Nothing.

So, what is my legacy, you ask?

Sure, I want to change the world.

Yes, I want FoxPoint to survive for many years after I am gone.

I want to build up authentic leaders that build up authentic leaders…that build up…you get the idea.

With all that said, my number one legacy is still my family.

I lead my three children and my wife in this world, and I pray they will follow me every day.

I want them to look at me and see that I am *a leader worth following*. I want them to go out and change the world. And in the end, know that I honored my grandfather's call to action and that I took care of my family.

First.

Always.

Forever.

In closing, here are *five keys* to solidifying the legacy of *a leader worth following:*

1. Protect your name

The most important thing about you in your lifetime is your name. Work hard to make certain it is never besmirched or soiled. Keep it free from scandal. Too many great people in history failed to do that in their lifetime and it cost their legacy and reputation dearly.

 "Keep your name and your credit good, it will beat you to the next place."

2. Do the right thing

This is the how-to of ensuring point #1 above. If you are focused on always doing the right thing your name will always resonate excellence, integrity and a life worth following.

3. Serve others

Every person who has an honored legacy spent the core of their lives serving those around them in a variety of ways. You cannot have a great legacy if you live for yourself, much less be *a leader worth following.*

> **"At the end of life we will not be judged by
> how many diplomas we have received,
> how much money we have made,
> how many great things we have done.
> We will be judged by 'I was hungry,
> and you gave me something to eat,
> I was naked and you clothed me.
> I was homeless, and you took me in.'"**
> Mother Theresa

4. Keep your ego in check

No one admires a showoff, a braggart, a hothead or jerk. The most difficult thing for intelligent, talented and famous people to handle is *themselves.* Make sure you control your ego wherever you go. It will determine the success or failure of your legacy.

A prime example of this point is Woody Hayes, the legendary football coach of Ohio State University. In his stellar career, Hayes won five National

Championships and was inducted into the College Football Hall of Fame but he lost control of his ego and his temper in the 1978 Gator Bowl when Clemson linebacker Charlie Bauman intercepted a pass late in the game, preventing the Buckeyes from winning.

Hayes grabbed Bauman and slugged him in the throat. It was a momentary lapse of judgment, witnessed by a national television audience. All the accolades that Hayes had garnered were wiped out by one punch. He was fired the following week and never coached again.

His legacy?

I will give you three clues, Nixon, Elvis and OJ. Keep your ego in check or you will not be pleased at history's final verdict of your life.

5. Go the *extra* mile

The more you sacrifice, the more you extend greatness, the more you risk to make the world a better place the greater your legacy. Don't just pursue a goal, chase after great big dreams! That will be what makes your life different.

A leader worth following never seeks to be great. He or she strives to be honest, serve others and passionately spend their life to make the world a better place in the most unselfish and unassuming ways they can.

That's what makes them a leader. That's what makes them great. That is why they are worth following.

**Now, go work on your life and
your legacy will take care of itself.**

EPILOGUE

A leader worth following has a credo
that is founded on integrity:

"Live a life worth dying for."

Those six words sum up remarkable and admired leaders. It's not enough to exist nor is it satisfactory to just be a good company man or hold a key position in management.

A *real* leader, that people want to follow, is not only going somewhere they *are* the somewhere. They are character and morality in motion. They don't just lead their followers to goodness. They emanate the virtue from their soul.

I am not exaggerating here. These are the kinds of leaders that truly change the world. Over history, we have seen powerful personalities and dynamic dictators from Julius Caesar to Saddam Hussein but their ability to control and dominate the masses did not make them leaders worth following. It just made them infamous.

A great leader needs more than power. He or she needs a principled foundation at the core of their being. They say that, "power corrupts" but, the truth is no power has power unless the person using it *chooses* to be corrupt.

Most people in the world are followers, probably in the 90 percentile. That is why it is imperative for you as a leader to recognize the significance of influence not just for your own legacy but for the future of all those who believe in your leadership.

> **"Setting an example from the top
> has a ripple effect throughout
> a business school or a corporation.
> After nearly three decades
> in business, 10 years as chief executive
> of a Big Eight accounting firm,
> I have learned that the standards
> set at the top filter throughout a company."**
> Professor Thomas Dunfee of the Wharton School

It begins and ends at the top and the best way I can graphically describe this is a tale of two Generals.

Both graduated from the Military Academy at West Point, both were meticulous in their preparations for battle, both served admirably in wars and both were responsible for thousands of men.

But, the similarities stop there.

One of them, General Dwight D. Eisenhower, was the architect of D-Day and later served two full terms as President of the United States. He was *a leader worth following*.

The other, General George Armstrong Custer, distinguished himself in the Civil War but at the end of his life led his men into the Valley of the Little Big Horn getting all of them killed in the most notable massacre in history.

 **"Credentials do not equal character
when it comes to competence."**

The true measure of a leader who deserves a faithful following cannot be one-dimensional; it must include the depth and texture of integrity.

Every day you live your life you are building your name, your reputation, and your legacy. You are also becoming more or less worthy of a following. The choice is yours.

Throughout this book, I have attempted to show you what makes *a leader worth following,* or not. My hopes and dreams go with you as you ultimately decide who you are and whether people will follow you or not.

I leave you with one final thought to summarize this entire book:

**"Don't spend your precious time asking
'Why isn't the world a better place?'
It will only be time wasted.
The question to ask is
'How can I make it better?'
To that, there is an answer."** Leo F. Buscaglia

Get out there and be great.

The world is waiting for you...to be...

a leader worth following.

ACKNOWLEDGEMENTS

In case you didn't get the message and hear my passion, I believe strongly in the purpose of authentic leadership, having integrity and being someone worth following. This book comes from my heart with great thanks to God, my grandfather, my mother, my family and friends that are all leaders worth following.

There are also three people that without their professionalism, gifts, talents and time for the cause, this book simply doesn't happen. Thank you Pat Hurley, Dan Pongetti and Aurelie Krauss.

I need to thank each of you reading this right now. First, for buying this book and making a choice to spend time with me on this journey. Thank you for your desire to become a better person, a better leader and someone that is worth following.

You are why I get to do what I love to do, speak to thousands of people, train teams for improvement and share my heart through books because you support and believe in the message.

Thank you for who you are
and what you mean to the world!

Randy

NOTES

NOTES

NOTES

NOTES

Other books from Randy:

You have a dream.
You want to succeed.
Ignite your passion and uncover
the power and purpose of your leadership.
Live with a Soul on Fire!

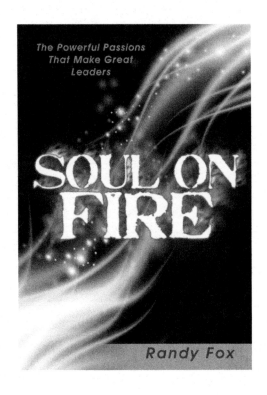

You want to grow,
to improve and to succeed.
Your progress depends on your principles.
Take the journey to dive deep into the simple,
yet effective, strategies needed to achieve results.

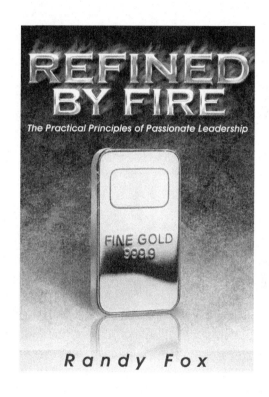

You need a game plan that is about achieving greatness
and sustaining success: together.
Time to turn your team, your workplace,
and your career into your dream come true.

You are better together than on your own!

At FoxPoint we recognize that your goal, your group,
and your event is unique.
We think your *speaker* should be too!

Randy customizes his presentations,
seminars, and workshops to meet *your* objectives.

Find out more at:

http://foxpoint.net

facebook.com/foxpoint

twitter.com/randy_foxpoint

linkedin.com/in/foxrandy

877.411.8498

As a professional speaker, author, and founder of FoxPoint, Randy Fox uses his leadership experience and energy to engage audiences and transform their leadership.

With a twenty-year career as a corporate leader and NCAA basketball official, Randy has a wealth of knowledge and a unique perspective on effective leadership. His focus is team-building and advocating for the potential in all workers in order to turn everyday people into superstar leaders. His leadership approach emphasizes interpersonal value systems and productivity, believing that from one the other naturally follows.

Randy is a professional member of the National Speakers Association, the author of several noteworthy leadership books, and has a number of prestigious television and radio appearances to his credit.

Randy enjoys living in the Chicagoland area with his wife and three children.